RAILROADS IN TH
50 STATES
Coloring Book

EDUCATIONAL!

GEOGRAPHY

READING SKILLS

FUN!

International Standard Book Number 1-931477-05-1

The Railroad Press
PO BOX 444-C
HANOVER, PA 17331

www.alco628.com

**TRP
Educational Series**

Book I: The Alphabet Train

Book II: Railroads in the 50 States

Book III: Children's Railroad
Learning & Activity Book

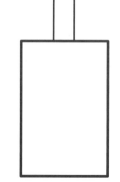

PRINTED IN THE UNITED STATES OF AMERICA.

NOTE TO PARENTS!

When your child finishes this book...

Thank you for purchasing the "Railroads in the 50 States"! We have published another book titled Children's Railroad Learning & Activity Book, which is the perfect companion book to the "Railroads in the 50 States". This 64-page book uses railroads and trains to teach valuable lessons about reading skills, math skills, geography, problem solving and learning to follow instructions! This book is available for $5.95 plus $1 shipping from the publisher. Our first book in this series, The Alphabet Train Coloring Book, is for younger children. They can ride along from A to Z as the train fills its cars with cargo that the children will love to color! Each page also has capital and small letters in different type styles so that children will be able to identify letters when they see them. It is available for $5.00 plus $1 shipping from the publisher.

WELCOME ABOARD!

The Fifty State Express

Let's climb aboard the "50 State Express" and travel around the country visiting every state! On our journey we will see train cars loaded with products going to or from each state. Cars are numbered in alphabetical order and many are decorated with symbols from their state flags. We will visit every state capital where we will learn when the state was admitted to the U.S. as well as its nickname, motto and symbols. We also will learn some of the names of the railroads that run in each state. We are ready to start our journey as the train pulls out of the station... next stop, Montgomery!

Alabama

22nd State admitted to Union:
December 14, 1819
Nickname: Heart of Dixie
Motto: We Dare Defend Our Rights
Tree: Southern Longleaf Pine
Bird: Yellowhammer
Flower: Camellia
RR's: BNSF, Norfolk Southern, CSX, Kansas City Southern

Montgomery

This flatcar is loaded with a dump truck that will be used at a bauxite mine in Alabama.

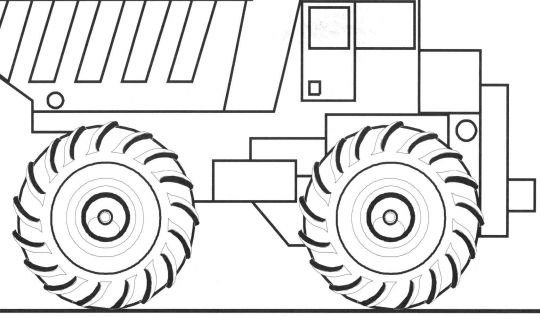

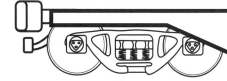

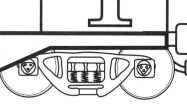

ALABAMA

Alaska

Juneau

49th State admitted to Union: January 3, 1959
Nickname: Last Frontier
Motto: North to the Future
Tree: Sitka Spruce
Bird: Willow Ptarmigan
Flower: Forget-me-not
RR: Alaska Railroad

This boxcar is loaded with fish from Alaska's rivers.

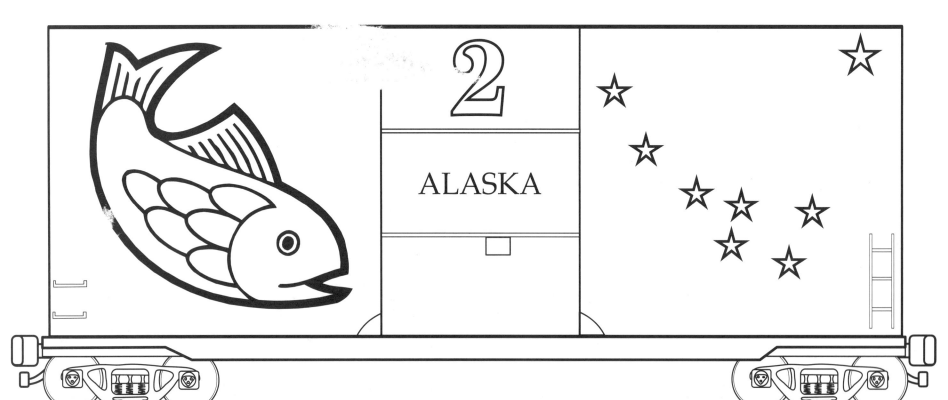

Arizona

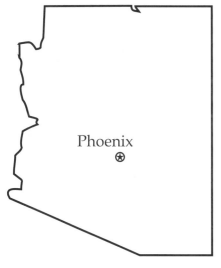

Phoenix ⊛

48th State admitted to Union: February 14, 1912
Nickname: Grand Canyon State
Motto: God Enriches
Tree: Palo Verde
Bird: Cactus Wren
Flower: White Blossom of the Saguaro
RR's: Burlington Northern Santa Fe, Apache,
Union Pacific, Copper Basin Railway, Magma,
San Manuel Arizona, Arizona Central,
Arizona Eastern, Arizona & California,
Black Mesa & Lake Powell

This car is loaded with gold ore from one of Arizona's many mines.

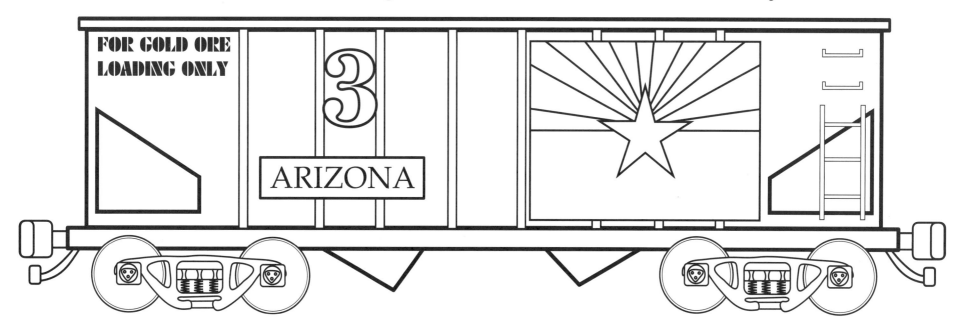

Arkansas

Little Rock ✪

25th State admitted to Union: June 15, 1836
Nickname: Land of Opportunity
Motto: The People Rule
Tree: Pine
Bird: Mockingbird
Flower: Apple Blossom
RR's: Union Pacific, BNSF, Arkansas & Missouri, Kansas City Southern

This boxcar is loaded with diamonds found in Arkansas mines.

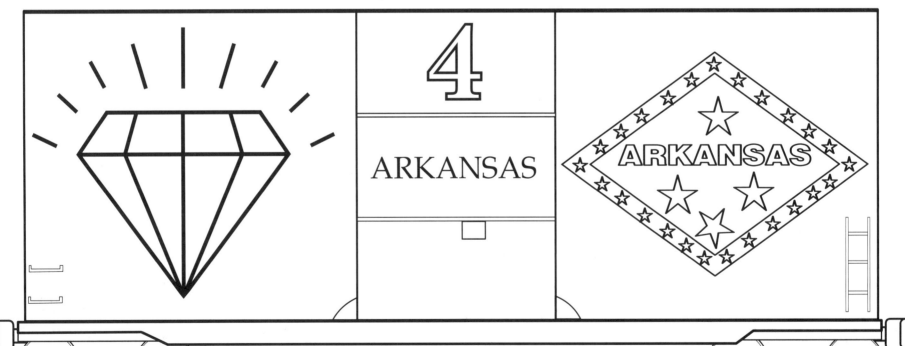

4
ARKANSAS

ARKANSAS

California

31st State admitted to Union: September 9, 1850
Nickname: Golden State
Motto: I Have Found It
Tree: California Redwood
Bird: California Quail
Flower: California Poppy
RR's: Union Pacific, BNSF

Sacramento

This tank car is filled with purple grape juice from the state of California.

5
CALIFORNIA

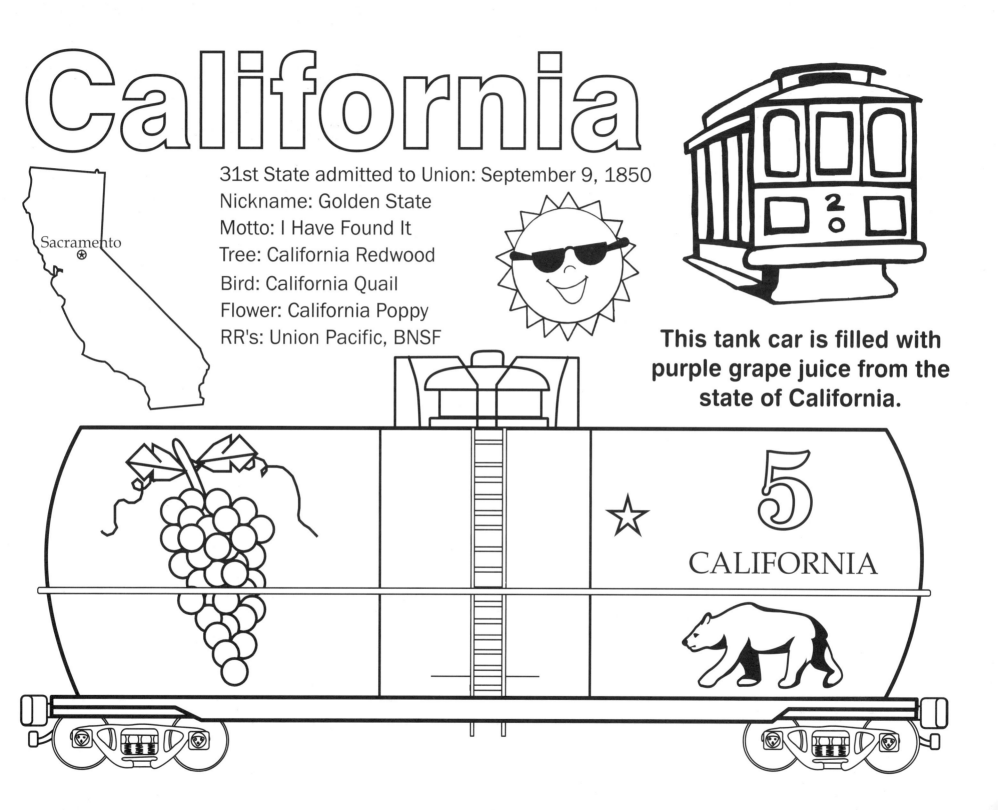

Colorado

38th State admitted to Union:
August 1, 1876
Nickname: Centennial State
Motto: Nothing Without Providence
Tree: Colorado Blue Spruce
Bird: Lark Bunting
Flower: White & Lavender Columbine
RR's: BNSF, Union Pacific, Kyle

Denver ✪

This boxcar is loaded with quarters from the Denver Mint.

Connecticut

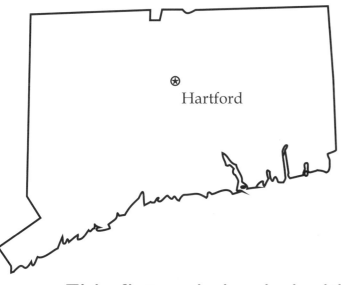

Hartford

5th State admitted to Union: January 9, 1788
Nickname: Constitution State
Motto: He Who Transplanted Still Sustains
Tree: White Oak

Bird: American Robin
Flower: Mountain Laurel
RR's: Guilford, Housatonic, New England Central, Providence & Worcester

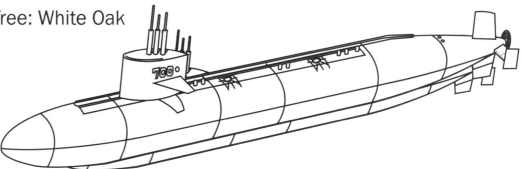

This flatcar is loaded with helicopters made in Connecticut.

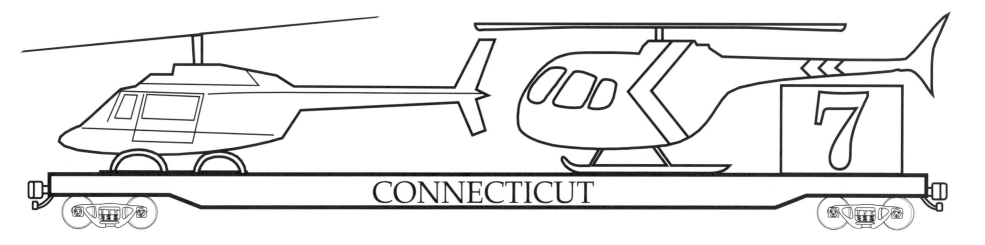

CONNECTICUT

Delaware

1st State admitted to Union: December 7, 1787
Nickname: First State
Motto: Liberty and Independence
Tree: American Holly
Bird: Blue Hen Chicken
Flower: Peach Blossom
RR's: CSX, Norfolk Southern

Dover

This tank car is loaded with colorful paint manufactured in Delaware.

8

DELAWARE

DIAMOND STATE

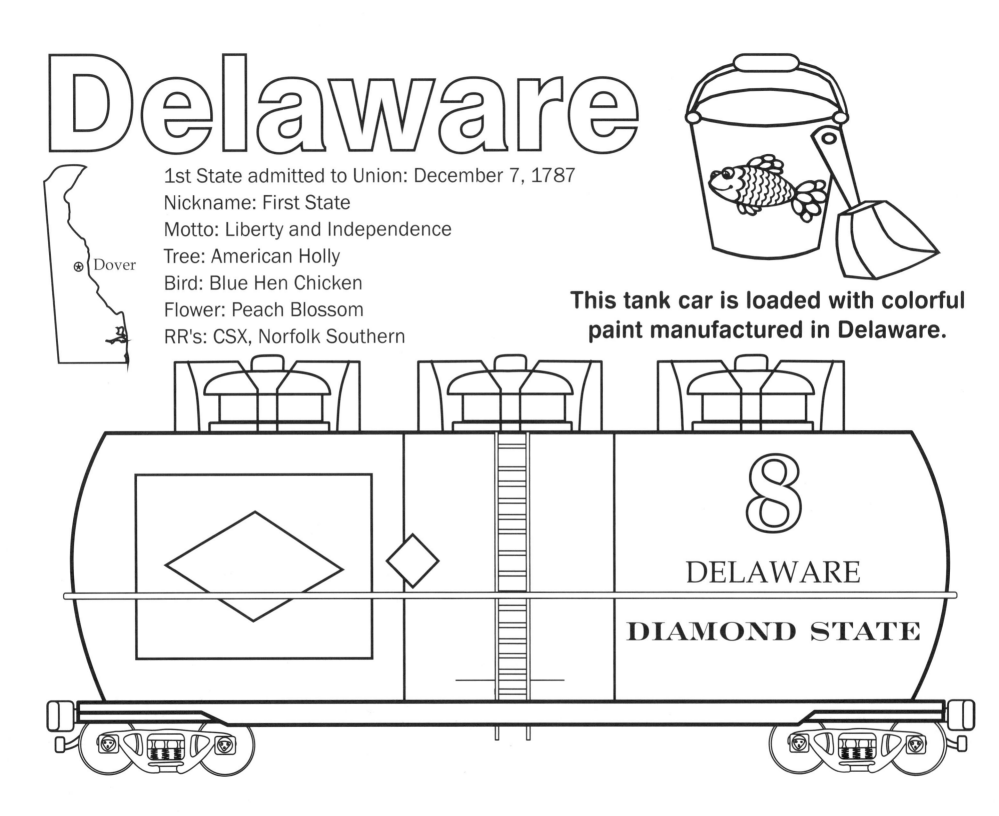

Florida

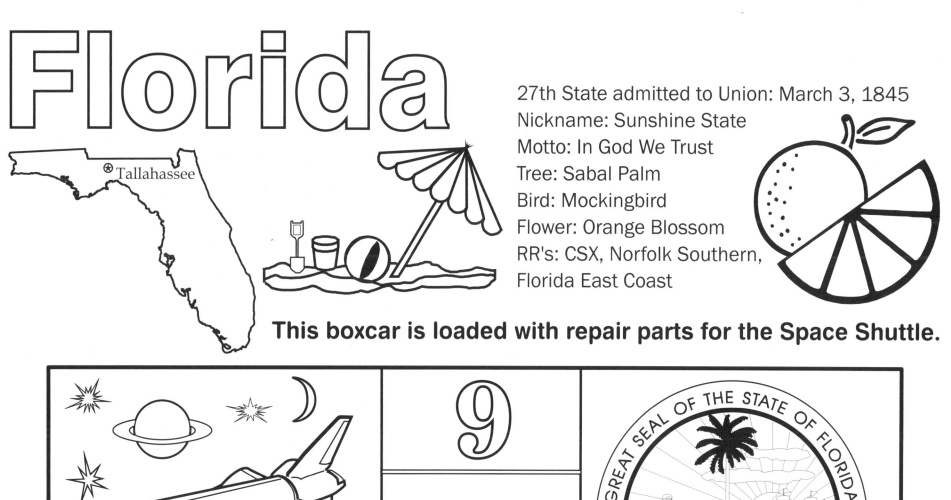

27th State admitted to Union: March 3, 1845
Nickname: Sunshine State
Motto: In God We Trust
Tree: Sabal Palm
Bird: Mockingbird
Flower: Orange Blossom
RR's: CSX, Norfolk Southern, Florida East Coast

Tallahassee

This boxcar is loaded with repair parts for the Space Shuttle.

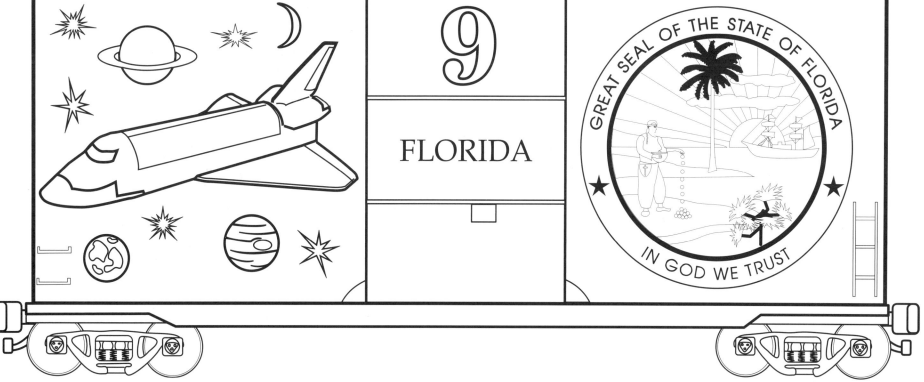

9

FLORIDA

GREAT SEAL OF THE STATE OF FLORIDA

IN GOD WE TRUST

Georgia

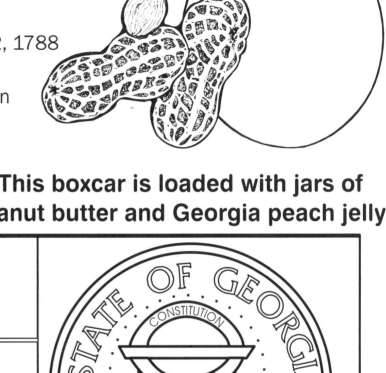

4th State admitted to Union: January 2, 1788

Nickname: Empire State of the South

Motto: Wisdom, Justice and Moderation

Tree: Live Oak

Bird: Brown Thrasher

Flower: Cherokee Rose

RR's: CSX, Norfolk Southern

Atlanta

This boxcar is loaded with jars of peanut butter and Georgia peach jelly.

PEANUT BUTTER

PEACH JELLY

10

GEORGIA

STATE OF GEORGIA

CONSTITUTION

JUSTICE

1776

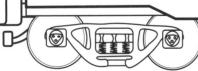

Hawaii

50th State admitted to Union: August 21, 1959
Nickname: Aloha State
Motto: The Life of the Land is
Perpetuated in Righteousness
Tree: Candlenut or "Kukui"
Bird: Hawaiian Goose or "Nene"
Flower: Yellow Hibiscus
RR: Lahaina, Kaanapali
& Pacific

Honolulu

This boxcar is filled with pineapples from Hawaii.

11

HAWAII

Idaho

Boise

43rd State admitted to Union: July 3, 1890
Nickname: Gem State
Motto: Let it be Perpetual
Tree: Western White Pine
Bird: Mountain Bluebird
Flower: Syringa
RR's: BNSF, Union Pacific,
Montana Rail Link,
Idaho Northern & Pacific

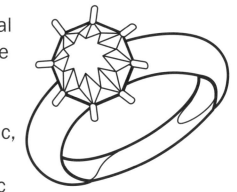

This boxcar is loaded with french fries made from Idaho potatoes.

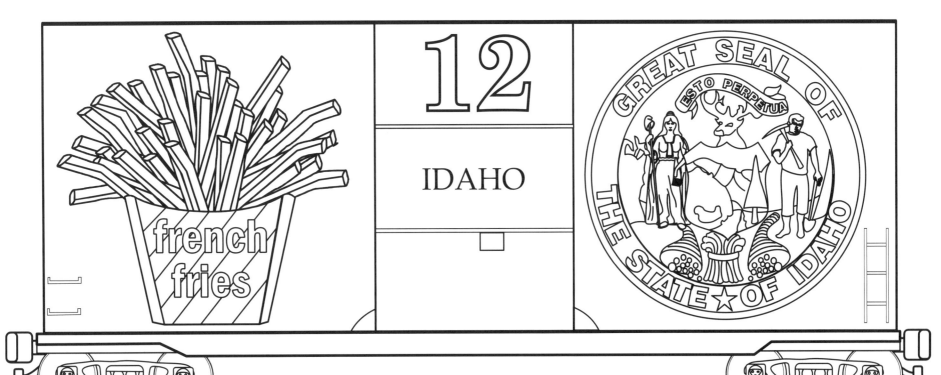

french fries

12

IDAHO

GREAT SEAL OF THE STATE OF IDAHO

ESTO PERPETUA

Illinois

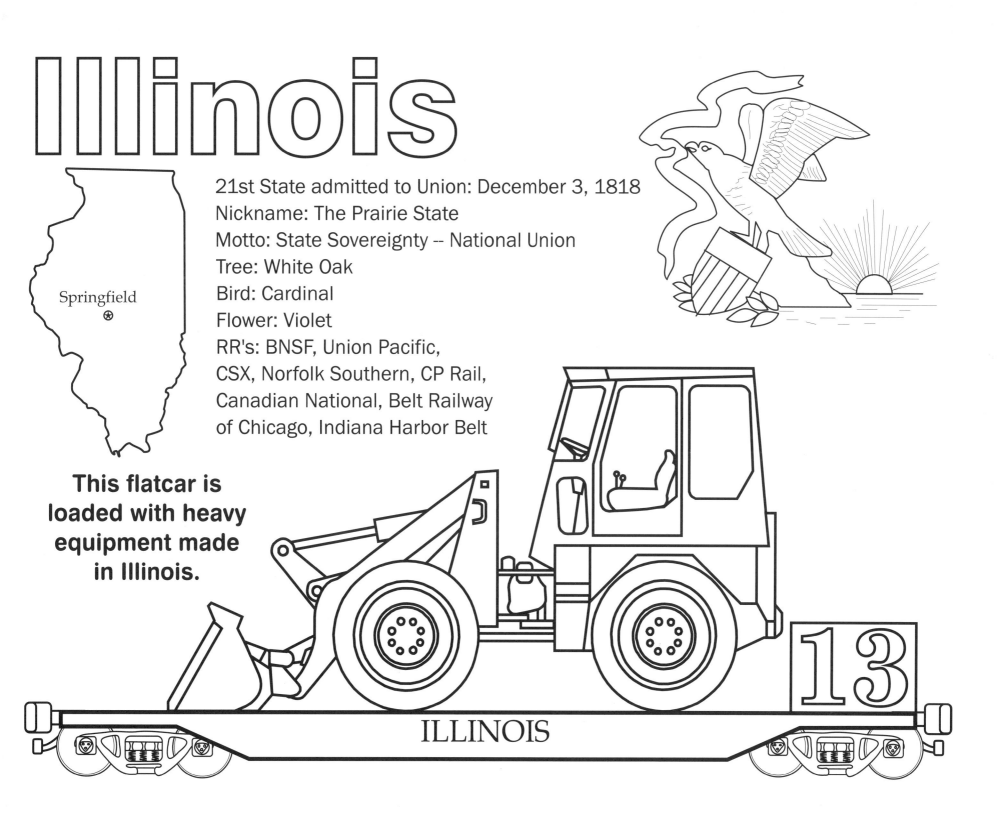

21st State admitted to Union: December 3, 1818

Nickname: The Prairie State

Motto: State Sovereignty -- National Union

Tree: White Oak

Bird: Cardinal

Flower: Violet

RR's: BNSF, Union Pacific, CSX, Norfolk Southern, CP Rail, Canadian National, Belt Railway of Chicago, Indiana Harbor Belt

Springfield

This flatcar is loaded with heavy equipment made in Illinois.

13

ILLINOIS

Indiana

19th State admitted to Union: December 11, 1816
Nickname: Hoosier State
Motto: Crossroads of America
Tree: Tulip Tree
Bird: Cardinal
Flower: Peony
RR's: Norfolk Southern, CSX, South Shore, Indiana Rail Road, Indiana Southern

Indianapolis

This auto carrier is bringing racing cars to the Indianapolis 500.

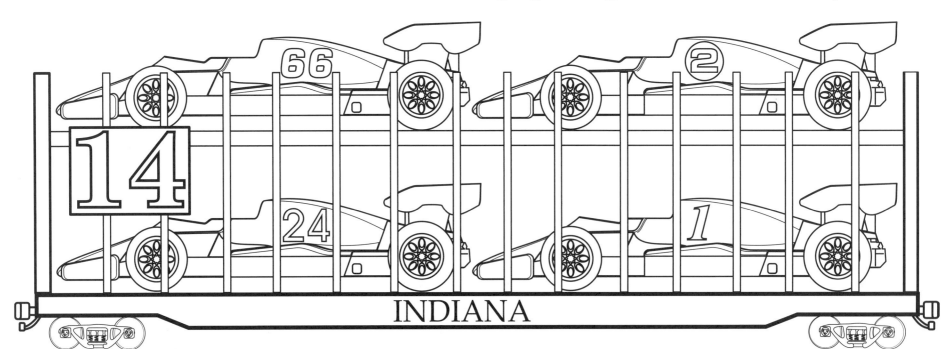

INDIANA

Iowa

Des Moines ✪

29th State admitted to Union: December 28, 1846
Nickname: Hawkeye State
Motto: Our Liberties we Prize and our Rights we will Maintain
Tree: Oak
Bird: Eastern Goldfinch
Flower: Wild Rose
RR's: BNSF, Union Pacific, Iowa Interstate, I&M Rail Link, Iowa Northern

This car is loaded with frozen food grown and packaged in Iowa.

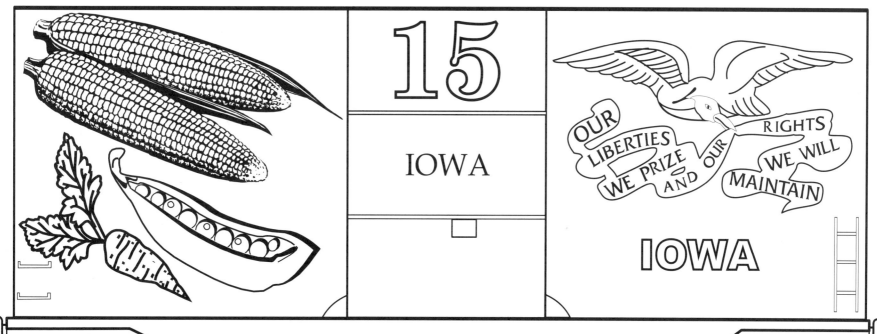

15

IOWA

OUR LIBERTIES WE PRIZE AND OUR RIGHTS WE WILL MAINTAIN

IOWA

Kansas

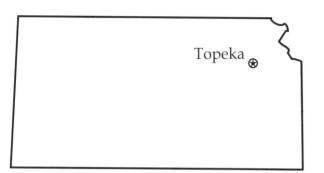
Topeka ⊛

34th State admitted to Union: January 29, 1861
Nickname: Sunflower State
Motto: To the Stars Through Difficulty
Tree: Cottonwood
Bird: Western Meadowlark
Flower: Native Sunflower
RR's: Union Pacific, BNSF, Kyle, Central Kansas

This boxcar is loaded with sunflower seeds from the fields of Kansas.

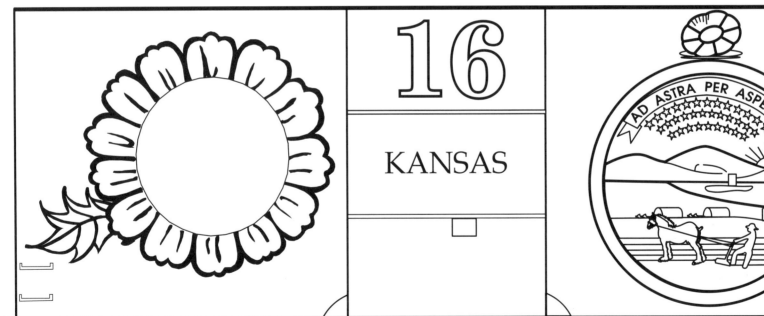

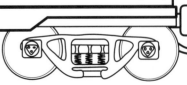

Kentucky

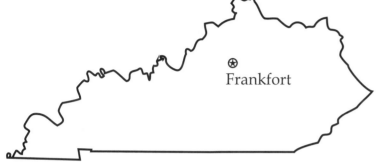

Frankfort

15th State admitted to Union: June 1, 1792
Nickname: Bluegrass State
Motto: United We Stand, Divided We Fall
Tree: Tulip Poplar

Bird: Cardinal
Flower: Goldenrod
RR's: CSX, Norfolk Southern, Canadian National, Paducah & Louisville

This boxcar is loaded with baseball bats from Kentucky.

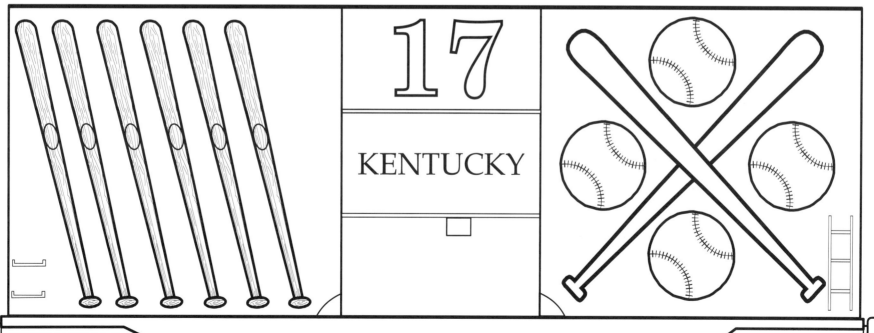

17

KENTUCKY

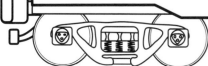

Louisiana

Baton Rouge ⊛

18th State admitted to Union: April 30, 1812

Nickname: Pelican State

Motto: Union, Justice, Confidence

Tree: Cypress

Bird: Eastern Brown Pelican

Flower: Magnolia

RR's: CSX, NS, KCS, UP, CN

This boxcar is loaded with jazz instruments heading for Louisiana.

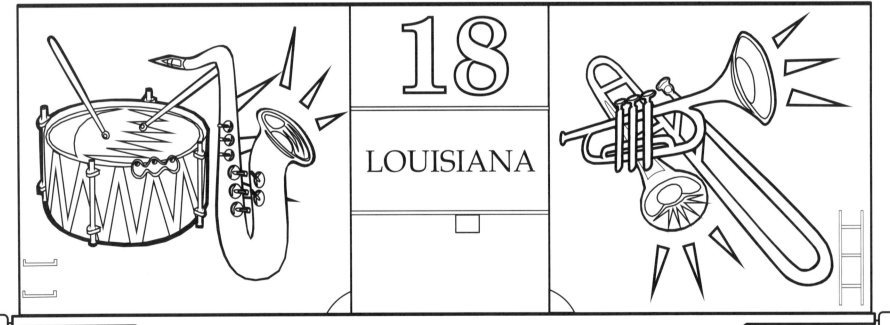

18

LOUISIANA

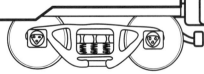

Maine

23rd State admitted to Union: March 15, 1820

Nickname: Pine Tree State

Motto: I Direct

Tree: White Pine

Bird: Chickadee

Flower: White Pine Cone and Tassel

RR's: Guilford, Iron Roads, St. Lawrence & Atlantic

Augusta

This boxcar is loaded with Maine lobsters.

19

MAINE

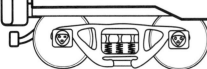

Maryland

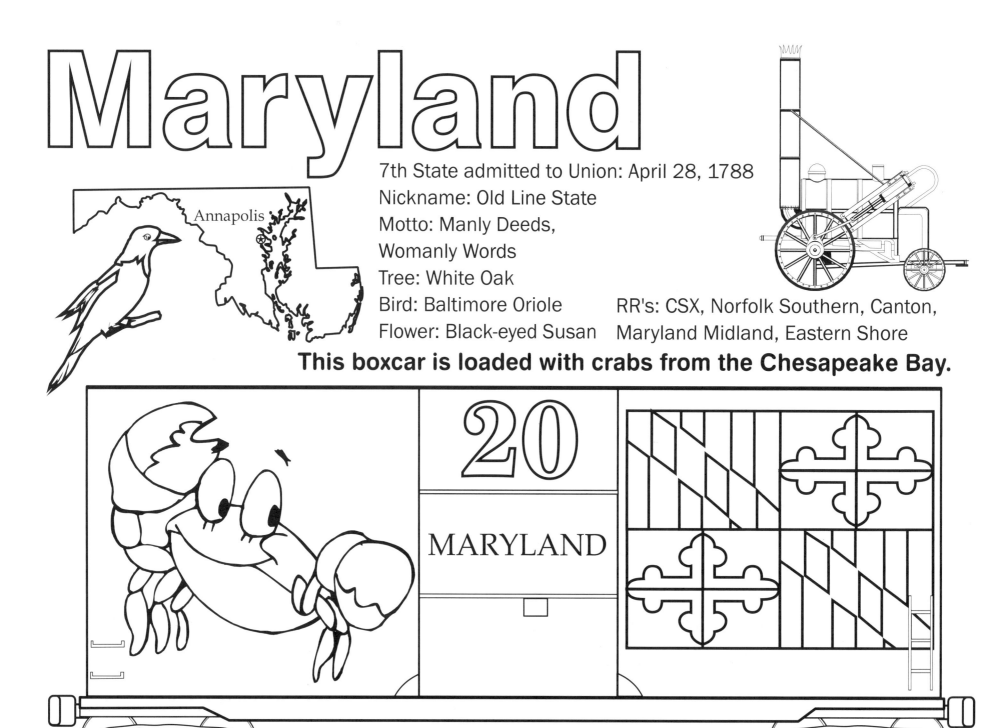

7th State admitted to Union: April 28, 1788

Nickname: Old Line State

Motto: Manly Deeds, Womanly Words

Tree: White Oak

Bird: Baltimore Oriole

Flower: Black-eyed Susan

RR's: CSX, Norfolk Southern, Canton, Maryland Midland, Eastern Shore

Annapolis

This boxcar is loaded with crabs from the Chesapeake Bay.

20

MARYLAND

Massachusetts

6th State admitted to Union: February 6, 1788

Nickname: Bay State

Motto: By the Sword We Seek Peace, but Peace Only Under Liberty

Tree: American Elm

Bird: Black-capped Chickadee

Flower: Mayflower

RR's: Pioneer Valley, CSX, Guilford, Bay Colony, New England Central, Housatonic

This tank car is loaded with cranberry juice made on Cape Cod.

Boston

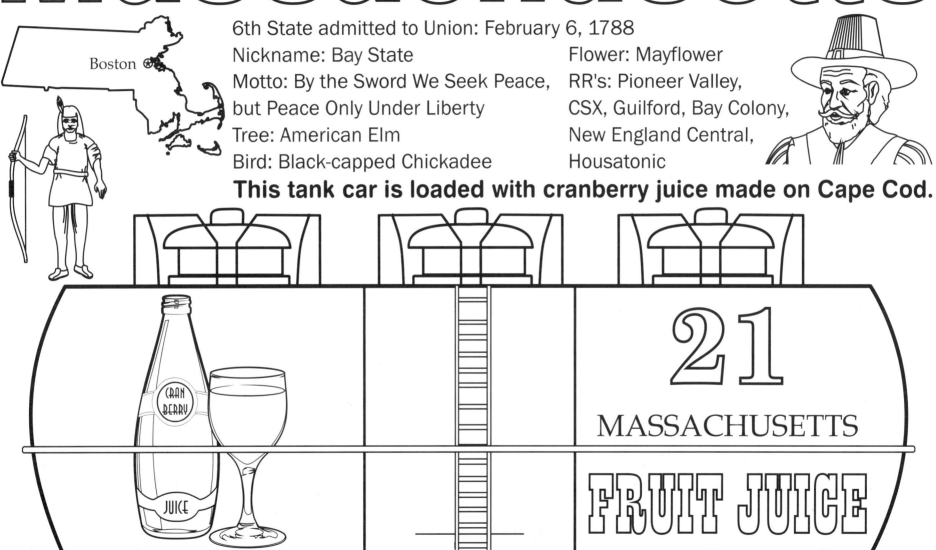

CRAN BERRY

JUICE

21
MASSACHUSETTS
FRUIT JUICE

Michigan

26th State admitted to Union: January 26, 1837

Nickname: Wolverine State

Motto: If You Seek a Pleasant Peninsula, Look About You

Tree: White Pine

Bird: Robin

Flower: Apple Blossom

RR's: CSX, Norfolk Southern, Lake State, Huron & Eastern, Lake Superior & Ishpeming, Ann Arbor, Tuscola & Saginaw Bay, CN

Lansing

This auto carrier is loaded with cars that were built in Michigan.

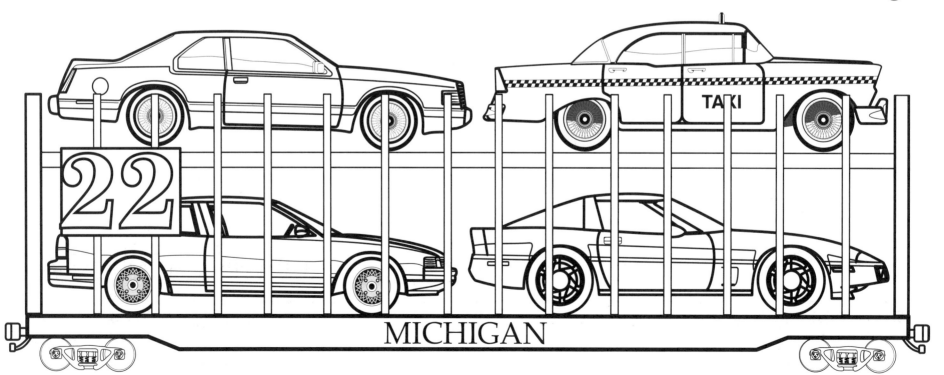

22

TAXI

MICHIGAN

Minnesota

32nd State admitted to Union: May 11, 1858
Nickname: North Star State
Motto: The Star of the North
Tree: Norway Pine
Bird: Common Loon
Flower: Pink and White Lady Slipper
RR's: Union Pacific, BNSF, Dakota, Minnesota & Eastern, Canadian National, Twin Cities & Western, Duluth, Missabe & Iron Range, Canadian Pacific

St. Paul

This car is loaded with purple taconite pellets which contain iron ore.

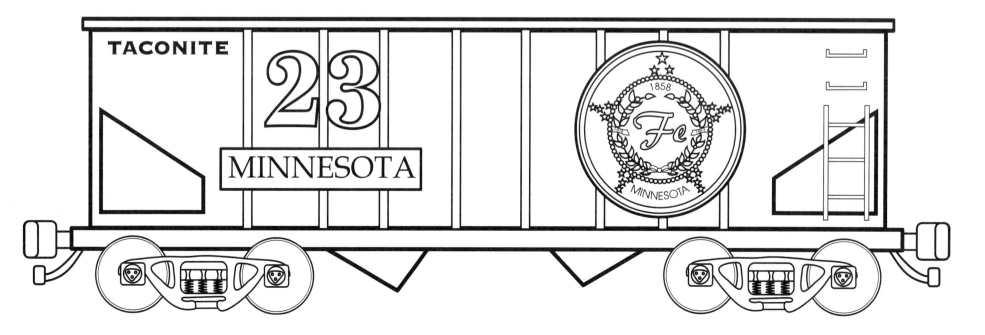

Jackson

Mississippi

20th State admitted to Union: December 10, 1817

Nickname: Magnolia State

Motto: By Valor and Arms

Tree: Magnolia

Bird: Mockingbird

Flower: Magnolia

RR's: BNSF, KCS, CN, NS

This boxcar is loaded with clothing made in Mississippi.

24

MISSISSIPPI

10

Missouri

Jefferson City ⊛

24th State admitted to Union:
August 10, 1821
Nickname: Show Me State
Motto: Let the Welfare of the
People be the Supreme Law
Tree: Flowering Dogwood
Bird: Bluebird
Flower: White Hawthorn Blossom
RR's: BNSF, Union Pacific,
Norfolk Southern, TRRA, I&M
Rail Link, Arkansas & Missouri

This gondola is loaded with heavy lead ingots from Missouri.

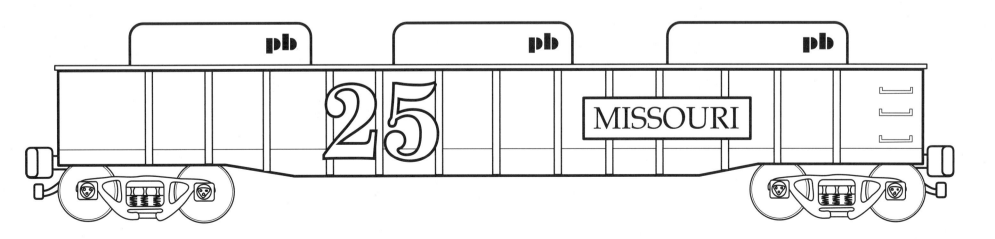

LEARN YOUR STATES!!!

Cover up the names in the right hand column.
Look at the number of the state that you are
guessing and then check to see if you are right!

1 ALABAMA
2 ALASKA
3 ARIZONA
4 ARKANSAS
5 CALIFORNIA
6 COLORADO
7 CONNECTICUT
8 DELAWARE
9 FLORIDA
10 GEORGIA
11 HAWAII
12 IDAHO
13 ILLINOIS
14 INDIANA
15 IOWA
16 KANSAS
17 KENTUCKY
18 LOUISIANA
19 MAINE
20 MARYLAND
21 MASSACHUSETTS
22 MICHIGAN
23 MINNESOTA
24 MISSISSIPPI
25 MISSOURI

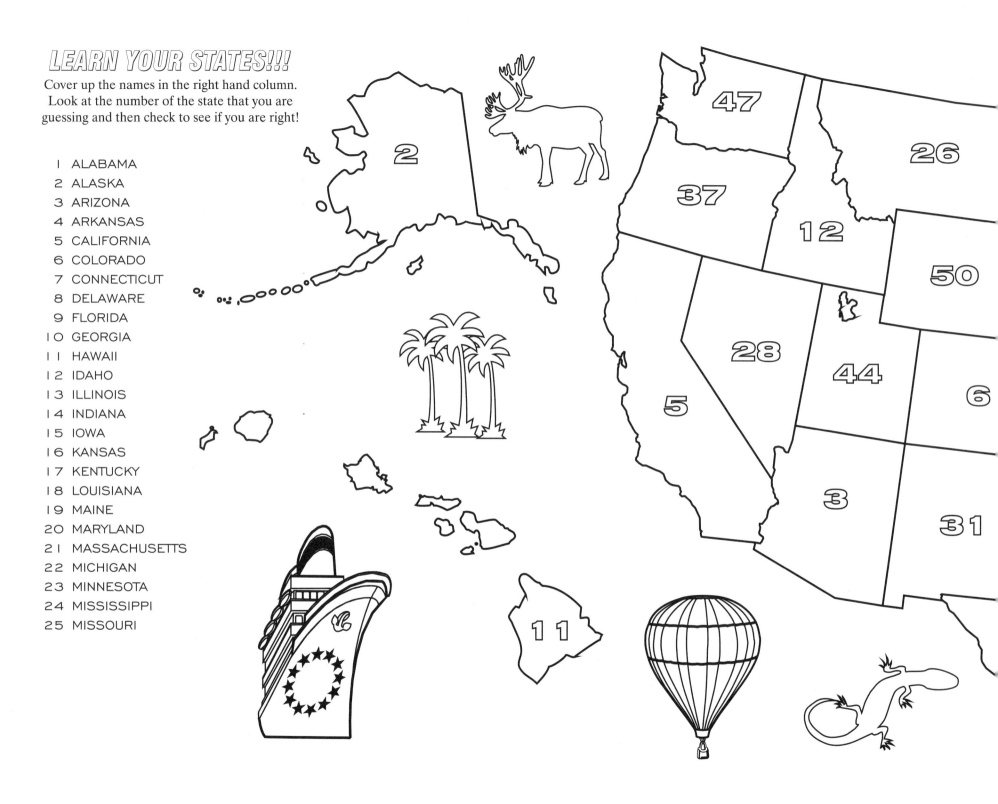

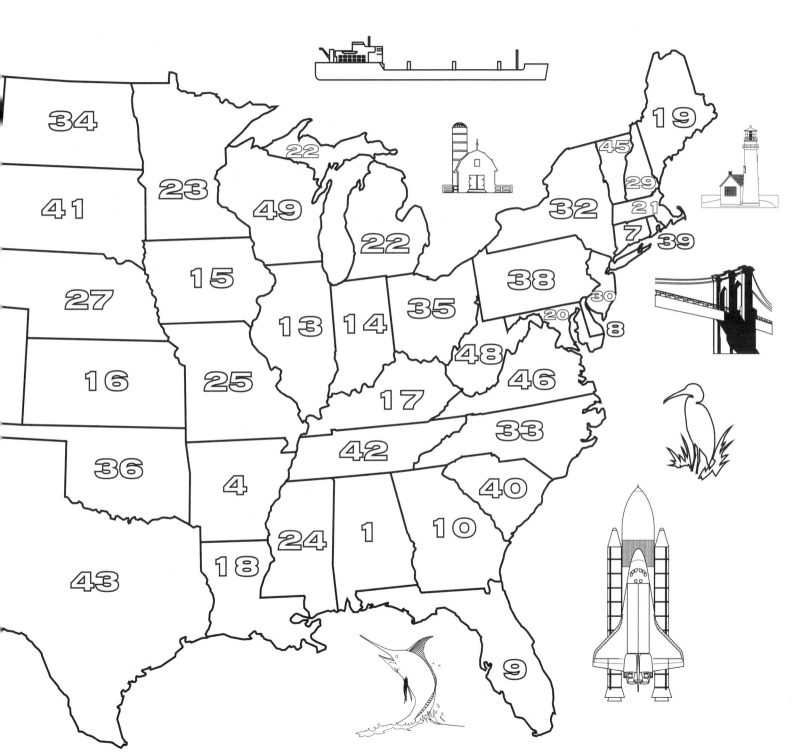

26 MONTANA
27 NEBRASKA
28 NEVADA
29 NEW HAMPSHIRE
30 NEW JERSEY
31 NEW MEXICO
32 NEW YORK
33 NORTH CAROLINA
34 NORTH DAKOTA
35 OHIO
36 OKLAHOMA
37 OREGON
38 PENNSYLVANIA
39 RHODE ISLAND
40 SOUTH CAROLINA
41 SOUTH DAKOTA
42 TENNESSEE
43 TEXAS
44 UTAH
45 VERMONT
46 VIRGINIA
47 WASHINGTON
48 WEST VIRGINIA
49 WISCONSIN
50 WYOMING

Montana

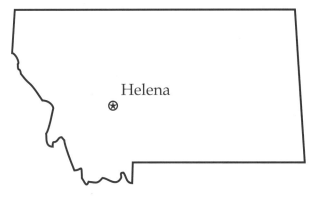

Helena

41st State admitted to Union:
November 8, 1889
Nickname: Treasure State
Motto: Gold & Silver   Flower: Bitterroot
Tree: Ponderosa Pine   RR's: BNSF, Montana Western,
Bird: Western Meadowlark   Montana Rail Link, Rarus

This flatcar is carrying a new transformer for a hydroelectric dam in Montana.

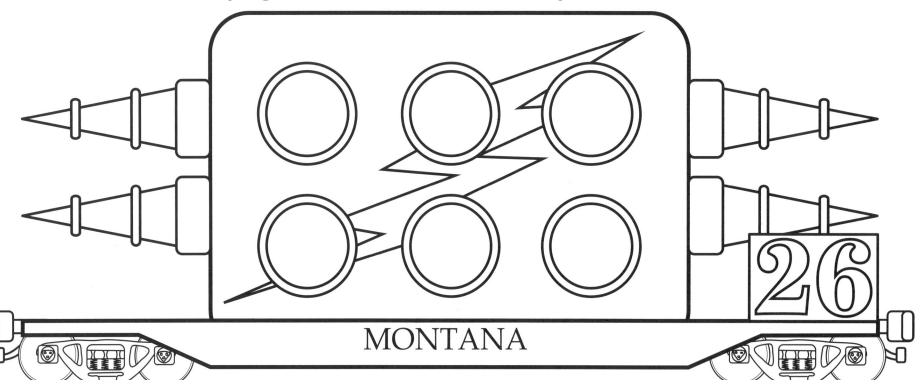

MONTANA

26

Nebraska

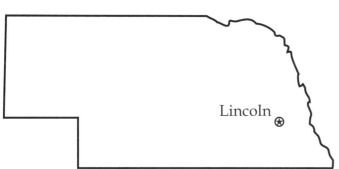

Lincoln ✪

37th State admitted to Union:
March 1, 1867
Nickname: Cornhusker State
Motto: Equality Before the Law
Tree: Cottonwood
Bird: Western Meadowlark
Flower: Goldenrod
RR's: Union Pacific, BNSF, Kyle, Nebraska Central, Nebkota

This car is loaded with corn grown on the plains of Nebraska.

27

NEBRASKA

GREAT SEAL OF THE STATE OF NEBRASKA
EQUALITY BEFORE THE LAW
MARCH 1 1867

Nevada

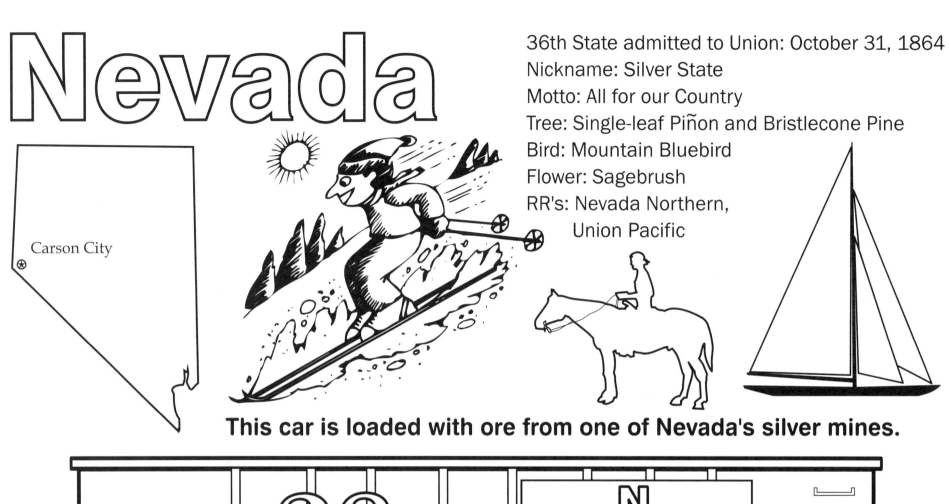

Carson City

36th State admitted to Union: October 31, 1864
Nickname: Silver State
Motto: All for our Country
Tree: Single-leaf Piñon and Bristlecone Pine
Bird: Mountain Bluebird
Flower: Sagebrush
RR's: Nevada Northern,
    Union Pacific

This car is loaded with ore from one of Nevada's silver mines.

New Hampshire

9th State admitted to Union: June 21, 1788
Nickname: Granite State
Motto: Live Free or Die
Tree: White Birch
Bird: Purple Finch
Flower: Purple Lilac
RR's: New England Southern,
Guilford System

Concord

This boxcar is loaded with paper from New Hampshire.

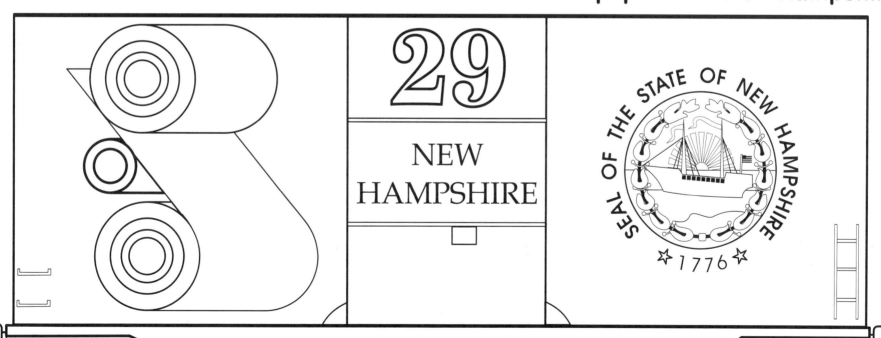

29

NEW HAMPSHIRE

SEAL OF THE STATE OF NEW HAMPSHIRE
1776

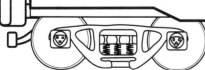

New Jersey

Trenton

3rd State admitted to Union: December 18, 1787
Nickname: Garden State   RR's: CSX,
Motto: Liberty and Prosperity   Norfolk Southern,
Tree: Red Oak   Morristown & Erie, Sou. RR of NJ,
Bird: Eastern Goldfinch   NY, Susquehanna & Western
Flower: Common Meadow Violet

This boxcar is loaded with soup made in New Jersey.

SOUP

30

NEW JERSEY

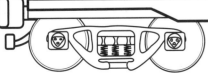

New Mexico

Santa Fe

47th State admitted to Union: January 6, 1912
Nickname: Land of Enchantment
Motto: It Grows as it Goes
Tree: Piñon Pine
Bird: Roadrunner
Flower: Yucca
RR's: BNSF, Union Pacific,
Santa Fe Southern, Southwestern

This car is loaded with potash, a fertilizer ingredient mined in eastern New Mexico.

31 NEW MEXICO

New York

Albany ⊛

11th State admitted to Union: July 26, 1788

Nickname: Empire State

Motto: Ever Upward

Tree: Sugar Maple

Bird: Bluebird

Flower: Rose

RR's: CSX, CP, Norfolk Southern, New York & Atlantic, Genesee & Wyoming, Livonia, Avon & Lakeville

This car is loaded with salt from deep mines in central New York.

SALT 32

NEW YORK

North Carolina

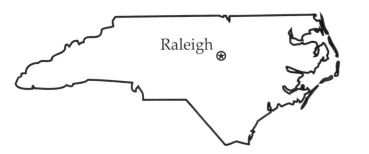
Raleigh

12th State admitted to Union: November 21, 1789
Nickname: Tar Heel State
Motto: To Be rather than to Seem
Tree: Pine
Bird: Cardinal
Flower: Dogwood
RR's: CSX, NS, Aberdeen & Rockfish

This boxcar is loaded with mackerel from North Carolina.

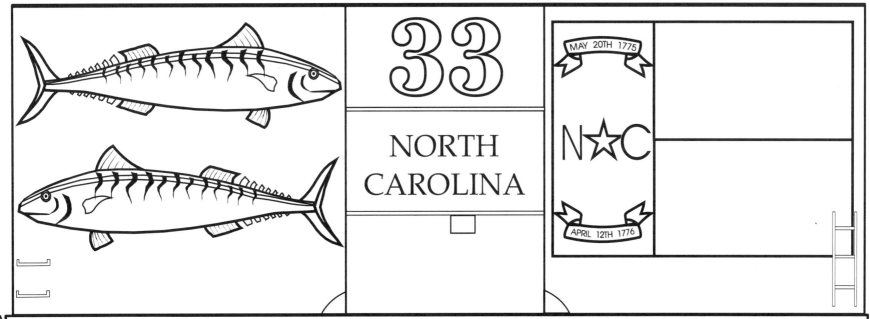

33
NORTH CAROLINA

MAY 20TH 1775
N☆C
APRIL 12TH 1776

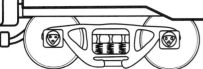

North Dakota

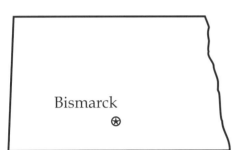

Bismarck ✵

39th State admitted to Union: November 2, 1889

Nickname: Peace Garden State

Motto: Liberty and Union, Now and Forever, One and Inseparable

Tree: American Elm

Bird: Western Meadowlark

Flower: Wild Prairie Rose

RR's: BNSF, Northern Plains, Red River Valley & Western, CP Rail

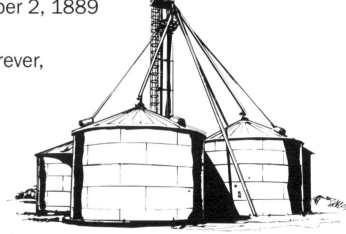

This car is loaded with sugar made from North Dakota sugar beets.

34 NORTH DAKOTA   SUGAR   SUGAR

Ohio

Columbus ✪

17th State admitted to Union:
March 1, 1803
Nickname: Buckeye State
Motto: With God, All Things are Possible
Tree: Ohio Buckeye (American Horsechestnut)
Bird: Cardinal
Flower: Red Carnation
RR's: CSX, Norfolk Southern, Ohio Central,
Wheeling & Lake Erie, Indiana & Ohio

This gondola is loaded with big industrial tires made in Ohio.

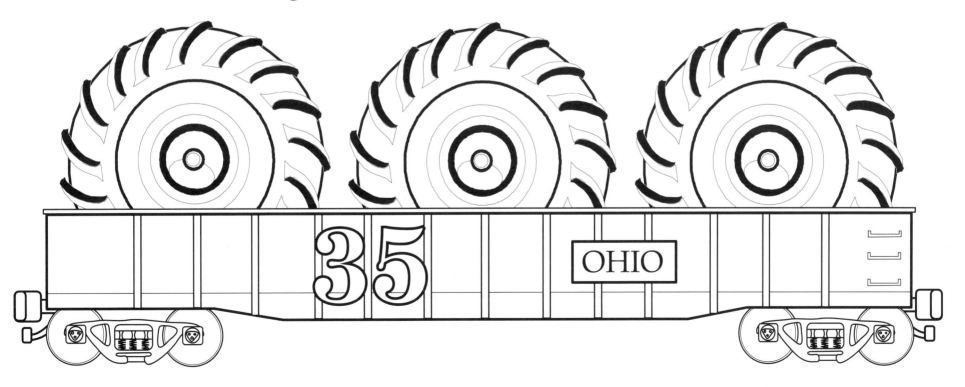

35   OHIO

Oklahoma

46th State admitted to Union:
November 16, 1907
Nickname: Sooner State
Motto: Labor Conquers
All Things
Tree: Redbud

Bird: Scissor-tailed Flycatcher
Flower: Mistletoe
RR's: BNSF, Union Pacific,
Farmrail, Tulsa-Sapulpa Union

Oklahoma City
⊛

This tank car is loaded with oil from wells in Oklahoma.

36

OKLAHOMA

CRUDE OIL

Oregon

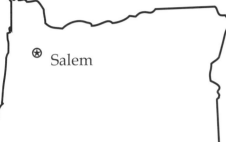

Salem

33rd State admitted to Union:
February 14, 1859
Nickname: Beaver State
Motto: The Union
Tree: Douglas Fir

Bird: Western Meadowlark
Flower: Oregon Grape
RR's: Union Pacific, BNSF,
Central Oregon & Pacific

This boxcar is loaded with lumber from the forests of Oregon.

Pennsylvania

Harrisburg ✪

2nd State admitted to Union: December 12, 1787

Nickname: Keystone State

Motto: Virtue, Liberty and Independence

Tree: Hemlock

Bird: Ruffed Grouse

Flower: Mountain Laurel

RR's: CSX, Norfolk Southern, CP, Reading & Northern, Bessemer & Lake Erie

This boxcar is loaded with crayons manufactured in Pennsylvania.

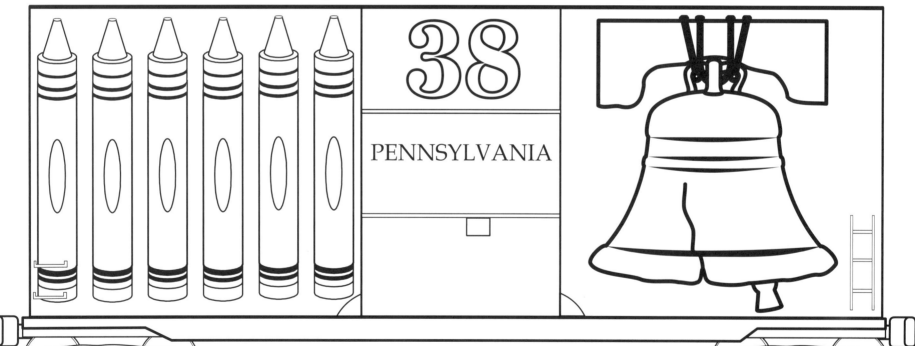

38

PENNSYLVANIA

Rhode Island

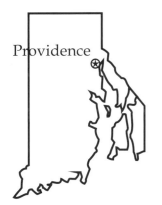

Providence

13th State admitted to Union: May 29, 1790
Nickname: Ocean State
Motto: Hope
Tree: Red Maple
Bird: Rhode Island Red
Flower: Common Blue Violet
RR: Providence & Worcester

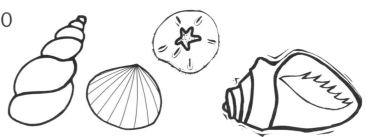

This boxcar is loaded with fishing equipment for fishermen in Rhode Island.

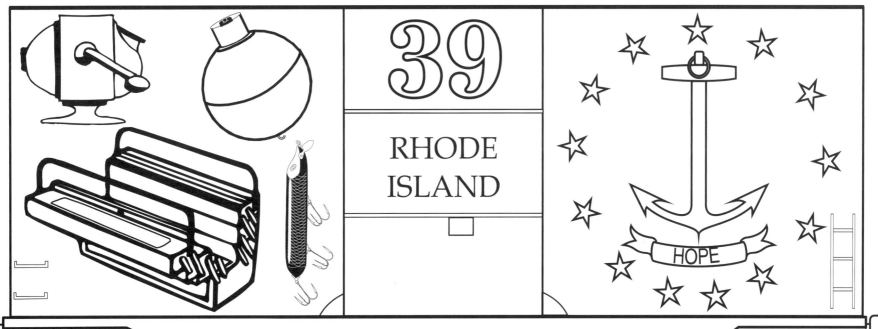

39

RHODE ISLAND

HOPE

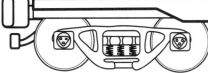

South Carolina

Columbia

8th State admitted to Union: May 23, 1788
Nickname: Palmetto State
Motto: While I Breathe, I Hope
Tree: Palmetto
Bird: Carolina Wren
Flower: Yellow Jessamine
RR's: CSX, Norfolk Southern

This boxcar is loaded with beach balls bound for the South Carolina seashore.

40

SOUTH
CAROLINA

South Dakota

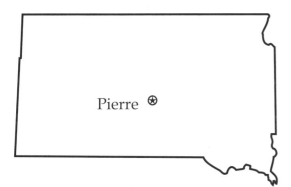

Pierre ✲

40th State admitted to Union: November 2, 1889

Nickname: Mount Rushmore State

Motto: Under God, the People Rule

Tree: Black Hills Spruce

Bird: Chinese Ring-necked Pheasant

Flower: Pasque Flower

RR's: BNSF, DM&E, Dakota Southern

This boxcar is loaded with bags of flour milled in South Dakota.

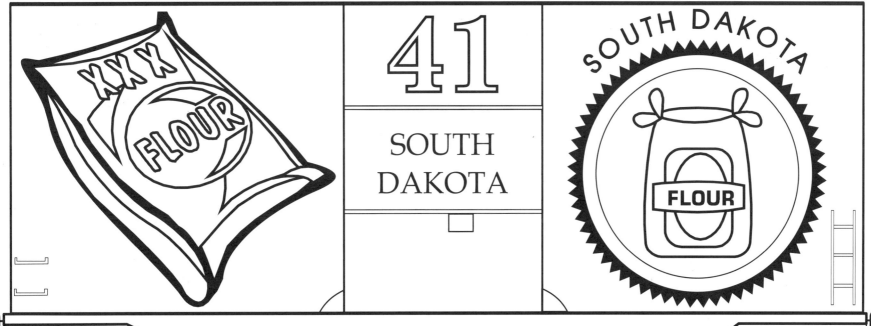

Tennessee

⊛ Nashville

This boxcar is loaded with fresh strawberries from Tennessee.

16th State admitted to Union:
June 1, 1796
Nickname: Volunteer State
Motto: Agriculture and Commerce
Tree: Tulip Poplar
Bird: Mockingbird
Flower: Iris
RR's: CSX, CN, Norfolk Southern, Nashville & Eastern

42

TENNESSEE

Texas

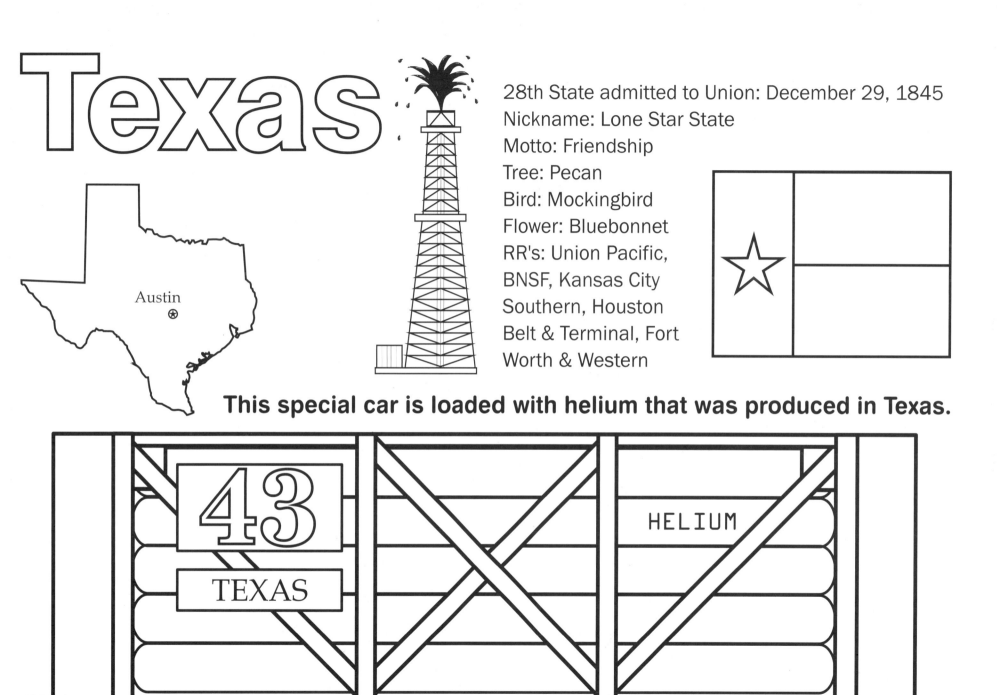

28th State admitted to Union: December 29, 1845
Nickname: Lone Star State
Motto: Friendship
Tree: Pecan
Bird: Mockingbird
Flower: Bluebonnet
RR's: Union Pacific, BNSF, Kansas City Southern, Houston Belt & Terminal, Fort Worth & Western

Austin

This special car is loaded with helium that was produced in Texas.

43
TEXAS
HELIUM

Utah

Salt Lake City

45th State admitted to Union:
January 4, 1896
Nickname: Beehive State
Motto: Industry
Tree: Blue Spruce
Bird: California Seagull
Flower: Sego Lily
RR's: Union Pacific, Utah Railway,
Salt Lake, Garfield & Western

This car is loaded with copper ore from Utah's Bingham Canyon.

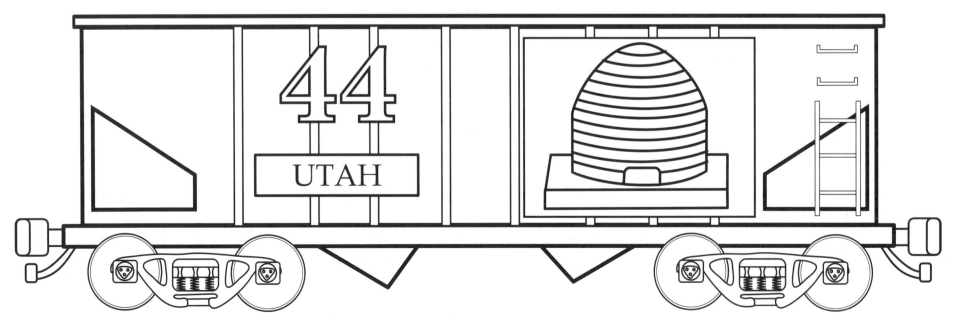

44

UTAH

Vermont

14th State admitted to Union: March 4, 1791

Nickname: Green Mountain State

Motto: Freedom and Unity

Tree: Sugar Maple

Bird: Hermit Thrush

Flower: Red Clover

RR's: Vermont Railway, New England Central

Montpelier

This tank car is loaded with pure Vermont maple syrup. Vermont is also known for its delicious ice cream!

45

VERMONT

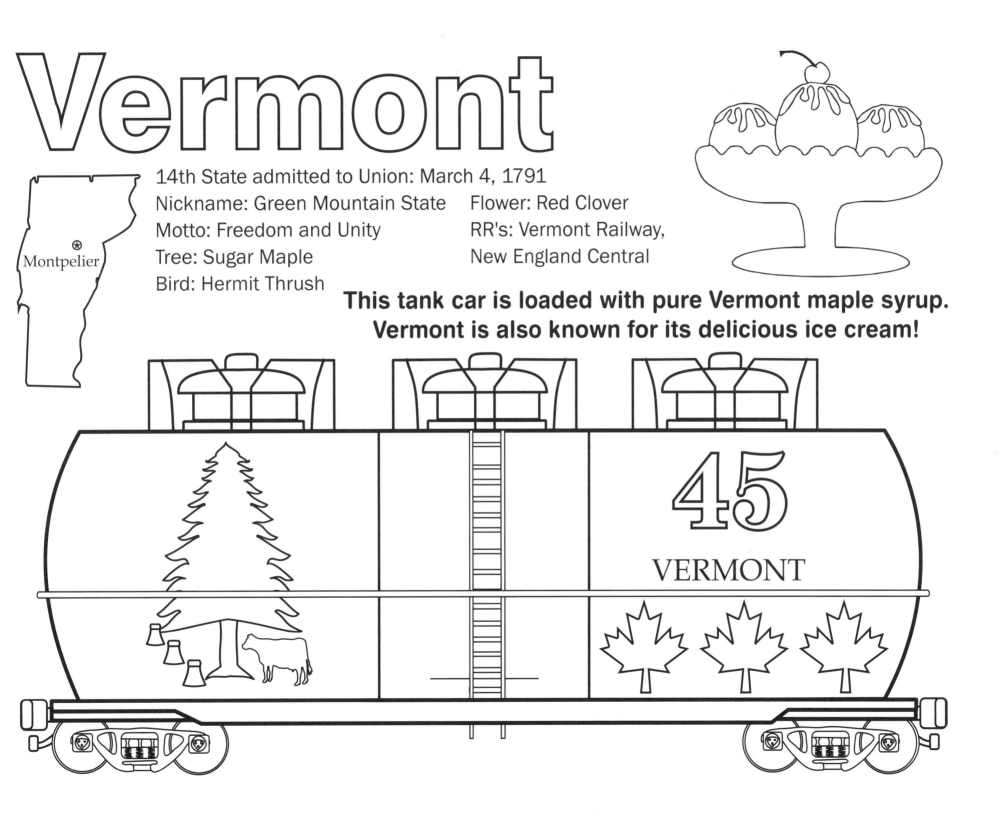

Virginia

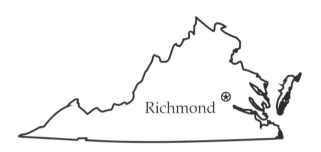

10th State admitted to Union: June 25, 1788
Nickname: Old Dominion
Motto: Thus Always to Tyrants
Tree: American Dogwood
Bird: Northern Cardinal
Flower: American Dogwood
RR's: CSX, Norfolk Southern, Winchester & Western

Richmond

This boxcar is loaded with parts for the Virginia shipyards.

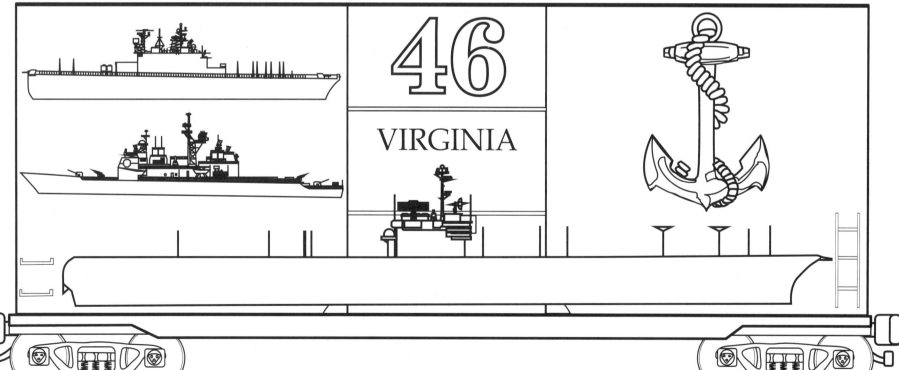

46

VIRGINIA

Washington

42nd State admitted to Union: November 11, 1889
Nickname: Evergreen State   Bird: American Goldfinch
Motto: By and By   Flower: Coast Rhododendron
Tree: Western Hemlock   RR's: BNSF, Union Pacific

Olympia

This boxcar is loaded with fresh apples from Washington orchards.

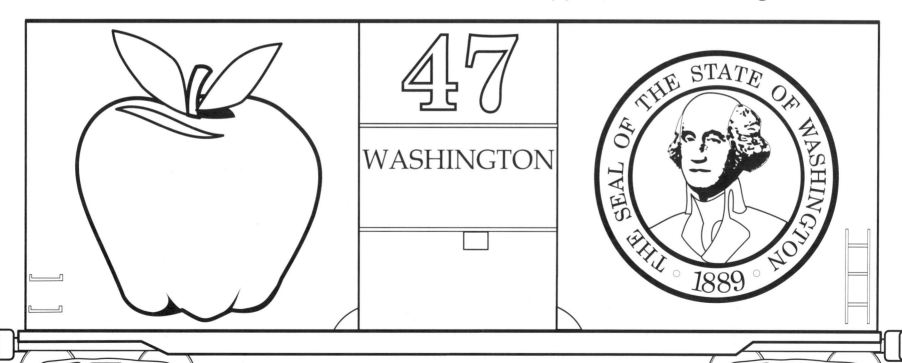

47

WASHINGTON

THE SEAL OF THE STATE OF WASHINGTON

1889

West Virginia

Charleston

35th State admitted to Union: June 20, 1863
Nickname: Mountain State
Motto: Mountaineers are Always Free
Tree: Sugar Maple
Bird: Cardinal
Flower: Rhododendron Maximum
RR's: CSX, Norfolk Southern

Coal mining is an important part of West Virginia's economy.

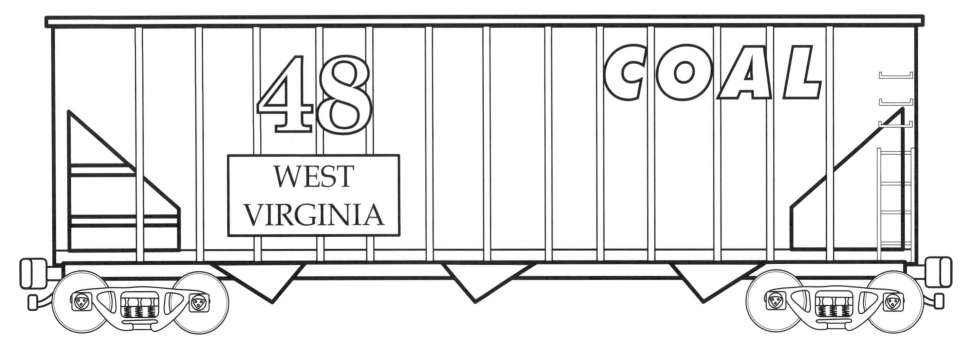

48

WEST VIRGINIA

COAL

Wisconsin

30th State admitted to Union: May 29, 1848

Nickname: Badger State

Motto: Forward

Tree: Sugar Maple

Bird: Robin

Flower: Wood Violet

RR's: BNSF, Union Pacific, Canadian Pacific, Canadian National, Wisconsin Southern, Escanaba & Lake Superior

Madison ⊛

This boxcar is loaded with dairy products from Wisconsin.

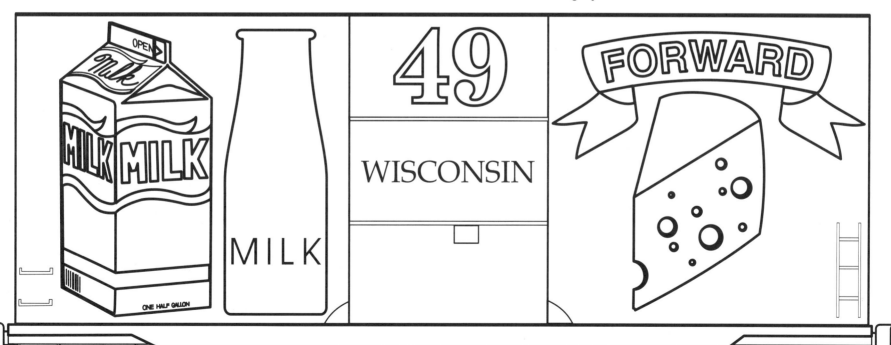

Wyoming

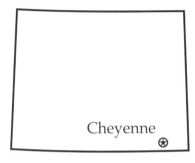

Cheyenne ✪

44th State admitted to Union: July 10, 1890
Nickname: Equality State
Motto: Equal Rights
Tree: Plains Cottonwood
Bird: Meadowlark
Flower: Indian Paintbrush

RR's: BNSF,
Union Pacific,
Wyoming & Colorado,
Bad Water Railway

This boxcar is loaded with cowboy hats going to Wyoming.

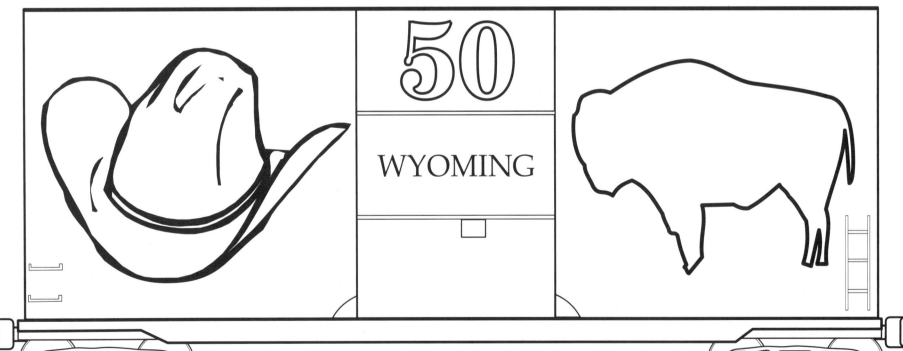

50

WYOMING

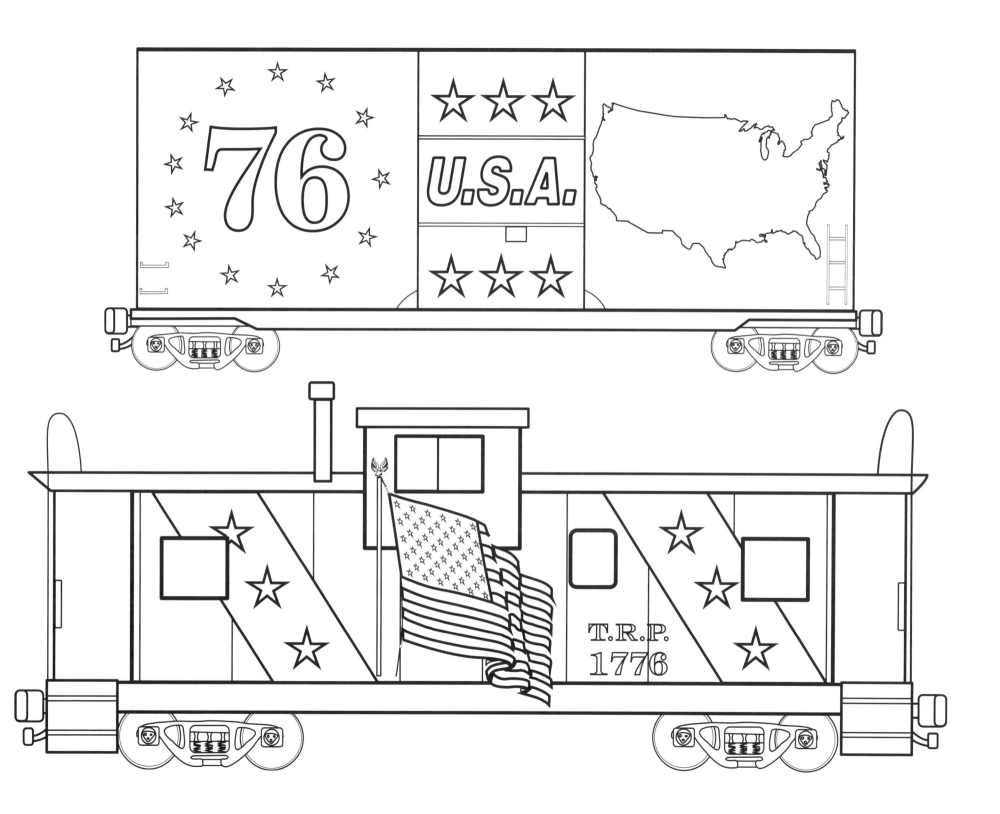

Do you remember in which states you found the following items?
Write the name of the state next to each item that belongs to it... good luck!

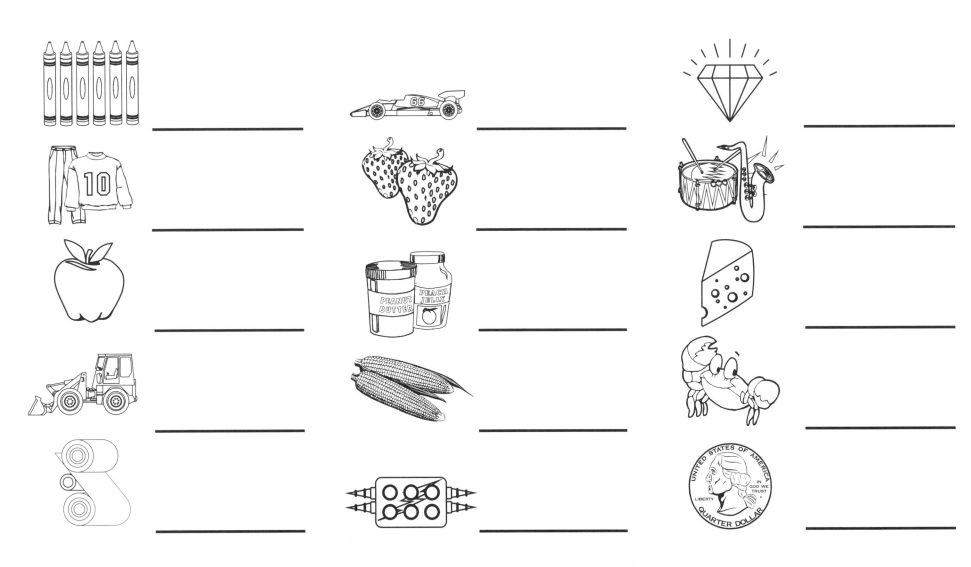

On the opposite page, write in the name of each state and then color the map.
Thank you for touring the 50 states by train. We hope you enjoyed your trip!